DISCARDED

EXCEPTIONAL ASIANS

BRUNO MARS

Singer and Songwriter

Kristen Rajczak
Nelson

E **Enslow Publishing**
101 W. 23rd Street
Suite 240
New York, NY 10011
USA

enslow.com

Words to Know

cover song—A song that is sung by anyone other than the original artist who recorded it.

debut—Having to do with someone's first appearance.

hula—A Hawaiian dance that uses the hands and the hips.

impersonation—Acting like another person, especially someone famous.

lyricist—Someone who writes the words to a song.

memorabilia—Important things having to do with a person or event, such as posters or clothing.

percussion—An instrument that is shaken or hit, like a drum.

platinum—An award given to albums that sell one million copies.

revue—A theater show that includes different songs and dances.

slum—A poor, dirty area, often in a city.

sound engineer—A person who works with different aspects of the music's sound.

Contents

Words to Know 2

CHAPTER 1   Childhood on Stage 5

CHAPTER 2   Hard Years 8

CHAPTER 3   Making Real Music 12

CHAPTER 4   Bruno Makes It Big 16

Timeline 22

Learn More 23

Index 24

Bruno Mars

Childhood on Stage

Bruno Mars's path to performing was set before he was even born. His parents met at a nightclub where his father played **percussion** and his mother was a **hula** dancer. While from very different backgrounds, they both loved performing and music. Bruno's father, Peter Hernandez, was Puerto Rican and Jewish. His mother, Bernadette, was born in Manila, the capital city of the Asian country of the Philippines. She came to live in Hawaii with her family in 1968.

A Young Performer

Bruno was born in Honolulu, Hawaii, on October 8, 1985. He was named Peter Hernandez, after his father. As a small child, he was called "Bruno" because he was chubby and looked like the wrestler Bruno Sammartino. Bruno started performing with his parents when he was just a toddler! He did an Elvis **impersonation** with their band the

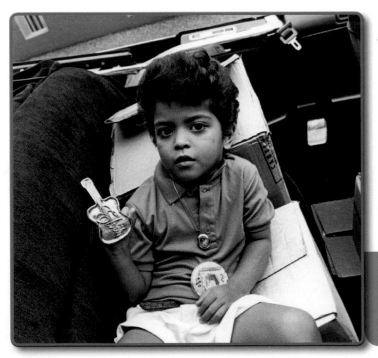

Love Notes. Then, Bruno had a small role as Little Elvis in the 1992 movie *Honeymoon in Vegas*.

Bruno at age four.

Bruno Says:

"Hawaii is basically in the middle of the world, so you're exposed to every type of music over there."

Bruno was hooked on making music right away. He found school boring compared to performing. His mother made him do chores, like keeping the dressing rooms clean. But Bruno just wanted to act like Michael Jackson and study other performers like James Brown. "It was like turning into Batman," he once said. "I'd go to school and kids are calling me Peter and we're playing baseball… and then—'All right, guys, I've got to go!'—you put on a sequined jumpsuit, and all of a sudden you're Bruno, the world's youngest Elvis impersonator."

CHAPTER 2

Hard Years

Bruno's earliest years were spent in the spotlight. His family performed two shows a night of mainly **cover songs** of doo-wop and music from the 1950s. Bruno learned to play drums, guitar, and piano. But when Bruno was about eleven, his parents divorced, and the family fell on hard times.

Bruno and his family moved to what he has called the **slums** of Hawaii. He had to start at a new school where no one knew him as a performing star. For a time, he was bullied there for how he looked. It was hard for Bruno to deal with his new life,

Bruno and Peter Hernandez sit together at an awards show. Bruno's father always encouraged his love of music.

especially when his father began to sell their Elvis **memorabilia** for money.

Finding His Way

Music remained important in Bruno's life through the tough years. His father bought him a guitar even when they had very little money. He taught Bruno to play songs by Chuck Berry and Carlos Santana. Peter Hernandez started another band and sometimes Bruno would sing with them.

By high school, Bruno had started to enjoy more modern music, especially songs produced by Timbaland and the Neptunes. He sang Ginuwine's "Pony" at a school assembly and started doing a Michael Jackson impersonation. Bruno made $75 a show opening for a local magic show. He saw that he could do more than impersonate, though, and began to dream bigger than the Hawaii music **revues** and cover bands.

Bruno Says:

"For me, music is 'I want to feel good' or 'I want to dance,' as opposed to me singing about me growing up in Hawaii and 'my struggle to relate.'"

Bruno grew up in the Waikiki city of Honolulu (shown here). After his parents' divorce, Bruno had to move to a poorer neighborhood.

Right after he graduated high school, Bruno moved to Los Angeles, California, to become a performer.

CHAPTER 3

Making Real Music

Bruno describes his early days in Los Angeles as "culture shock"—and not just because Hawaii had no billboards and LA is full of them. In Hawaii, race was never much of an issue for Bruno. But as a performer in LA, being half Puerto Rican and half Filipino confused people on where he might fit in the music scene. He was performing as Bruno Hernandez, making people expect Latin music from him. Soon Bruno took on the stage name "Mars."

Bruno worked hard at other jobs in the music business before he found success as a singer.

Writer and Producer

Motown, a famous record label, signed Bruno in 2004. He didn't record anything for them. However, through this deal he met Philip Lawrence, a **lyricist**. At this point, Bruno realized if he wanted to record the kind of music he liked, he'd have to start writing it himself. He and Philip began to work together with the hopes of getting Bruno another record deal. After awhile, they started working with a **sound engineer** named Ari Levine. Soon the three

13

men were writing and producing songs for other performers.

The trio, known as the Smeezingtons, worked with Brandy, Flo Rida, and other big names. Then, in 2009, Bruno sang on two huge hits the Smeezingtons wrote and produced—"Nothin' on You" with B.o.B.

Bruno Says:

"Being so young when I was first signed, I never really had a sense of who I wanted to be. Now things are really working out because everything that I'm singing, writing and composing is really me."

Bruno learned a great deal about making original music from working with the Smeezingtons. Bruno is seen here with Philip Lawrence (left) and Ari Levine.

and "Billionaire" with Travie McCoy. Suddenly, Bruno was getting noticed as a performer, not just a songwriter and producer!

Bruno Makes It Big

With the help of the Smeezingtons, Bruno was ready to make the music he always wanted to. After his introduction on the B.o.B. and Travie McCoy songs, Bruno was in demand. He signed with Elektra, another record label. In 2010, Bruno released an EP called *It's Better If You Don't Understand,* followed by a full album.

Doo-Wops & Hooligans, the Bruno Mars **debut** album, contained hints of Bruno's background singing songs from the 1950s, mixed with the hip-hop feel of the Smeezingtons. The album was a hit

Bruno found that in order to make the music he wanted to, he'd have to write it himself—so he did, with great success.

and went **platinum** thirty-nine times! The single "Just the Way You Are" went platinum twelve times and won Bruno his first Grammy Award for Best Male Pop Vocal Performance. Bruno finally had the spotlight of fame directed on him as he went on tour and made countless TV appearances.

As Bruno became more famous, he appeared on lots of TV and radio programs, like the one here in 2012.

Bruno Says:

It's hard to put myself in a box. I just write songs that I strongly believe in and that are coming from inside. There's no tricks. It's honesty with big melodies.

Superstar

In 2012, Bruno's second hit album was released. On *Unorthodox Jukebox*, Bruno continued to work with the other members of the Smeezingtons as well as other big producers such as Mark Ronson and Diplo.

Millions of people watch the Super Bowl on TV every year. Bruno's 2016 performance may have been his biggest so far!

Including the hit single "Locked Out of Heaven," *Unorthodox Jukebox* earned Bruno his second Grammy, winning for Best Pop Vocal Album.

Since then, Bruno performed as part of the halftime show at Super Bowl XLVIII in 2014 and Super Bowl 50 in 2016. He and Mark Ronson released "Uptown Funk," one of the biggest singles of 2015. And yet Bruno continues to work hard, rehearsing with his live band as much as possible before a tour: "We finally get to enjoy all the hard work that we've done when we play and when we sing."

Timeline

1985—Peter "Bruno" Hernandez is born on October 8.

1992—Has a small role in *Honeymoon in Vegas*.

2004—Signs with Motown. Meets Philip Lawrence and, with Ari Levine, becomes part of the producing group the Smeezingtons.

2009—Signs with Elektra.

2010—Releases *It's Better If You Don't Understand* and *Doo-Wops & Hooligans*.

2011—Wins first Grammy for Best Male Pop Vocal Performance.

2012—*Unorthodox Jukebox* comes out.

2013—Is named Artist of the Year by *Billboard* magazine.

2014—Performs at the Super Bowl halftime show.

2015—released "Uptown Funk" with Mark Ronson.

2016—Performs at the Super Bowl halftime show with Beyoncé and Coldplay.

Learn More

Books

Hibbert, Clare. *Pop Star*. Mankato, MN: Sea-to-Sea Publications, 2012.

Jimenez, Gidget. *All About the Philippines: Stories, Songs, Crafts, and Games for Kids*. Rutland, VT: Tuttle Publishing, 2015.

MacKay, Jenny. *The Art of Songwriting*. Detroit, MI: Lucent Books, 2014.

Watson, Stephanie. *Bruno Mars: Pop Superstar*. Minneapolis, MN: ABDO, 2014.

Websites

brunomars.com
Find out when Bruno Mars is touring and other news about his music!

grammy.com/artist/bruno-mars
See many photos and videos of the Grammy-winning Bruno Mars.

songwritingforkids.com/?section=news
Learn more about how you can write a song—and maybe even a hit!

Index

B.o.B., 15, 16

Doo-Wops & Hooligans, 16

Elvis, 6, 7, 9

Grammy Award, 18, 21

Hawaii, 5, 6, 8, 10, 12

Hernandez, Bernadette, 5, 7

Hernandez, Peter, 5, 6, 9

Honeymoon in Vegas, 6

It's Better If You Don't Understand, 16

Jackson, Michael, 7, 10

Lawrence, Phil, 13

Levine, Ari, 13

McCoy, Travie, 15, 16

music producers, 10, 14, 15, 19

Ronson, Mark, 19, 21

Sammartino, Bruno, 6

Smeezingtons, the, 14, 16, 19

songwriting, 13–14, 15, 19

Super Bowl, 21

Unorthodox Jukebox, 19, 21

Published in 2017 by Enslow Publishing, LLC.
101 W. 23rd Street, Suite 240, New York, NY 10011

Copyright © 2017 by Enslow Publishing, LLC.

Library of Congress Cataloging-in-Publication Data
Names: Nelson, Kristen Rajczak.
Title: Bruno Mars : singer and songwriter / Kristen Rajczak Nelson.
Description: New York : Enslow Publishing, [2017] | Series: Exceptional Asians | Includes bibliographical references and index.
Identifiers: LCCN 2015044480| ISBN 9780766078413 (library bound) | ISBN 9780766078475 (pbk.) | ISBN 9780766078093 (6-pack)
Subjects: LCSH: Mars, Bruno, 1985---Juvenile literature. | Musicians--United States--Biography--Juvenile literature. | LCGFT: Biographies.
Classification: LCC ML3930.M318 N45 2016 | DDC 782.42164092--dc23
LC record available at http://lccn.loc.gov/2015044480

Printed in Malaysia

To Our Readers: We have done our best to make sure all website addresses in this book were active and appropriate when we went to press. However, the author and the publisher have no control over and assume no liability for the material available on those websites or on any websites they may link to. Any comments or suggestions can be sent by e-mail to customerservice@enslow.com.

Photo Credits: Throughout book, ©Toria/Shutterstock.com (blue background); cover, p. 1 S Bukley/Shutterstock.com; p. 4 Kevork Djansezian/Getty Images; p. 6 Catherine McGann/Getty Images; p. 9 Kevin Mazur/WireImage for MTV/Getty Images; p. 11 NICHOLAS KAMM/AFP/Getty Images; p. 13 AP Photo/Keystone, Alessandro Della Bella; p. 15 Steve Granitz/WireImage/Getty Images; p. 17 Jeff Kravitz/FilmMagic/Getty Images; p. 18 Matthew Eisman/WireImage/Getty Images; p. 20 Ezra Shaw/Getty Images.